HANGMAN

PUZZLES

for Recess

JACK KETCH

JUNIOR

PUZZLE
WRIGHT
JUNIOR

JUNIOR New York

An Imprint of Sterling Publishing Co., Inc.
1166 Avenue of the Americas
New York, NY 10036

ISBN 978-1-4549-2713-6

Distributed in Canada by Sterling Publishing
c/o Canadian Manda Group, 664 Annette Street
Toronto, Ontario, Canada M6S 2C8
Distributed in the United Kingdom by GMC Distribution Services
Castle Place, 166 High Street, Lewes, East Sussex, England BN7 1XU
Distributed in Australia by NewSouth Books, 45 Beach Street, Coogee
NSW 2034, Australia

For information about custom editions, special sales, and premium and
corporate purchases, please contact Sterling Special Sales at 800-805-5489
or specialsales@sterlingpublishing.com.

Manufactured in China
Lot #:
2 4 6 8 10 9 7 5 3 1
07/17

sterlingpublishing.com
puzzlewright.com

RULES

Hello! You must be very brave.
Simply by opening this book you have chosen to play
a dangerous game: hangman. Your goal is to reveal
a word or phrase by correctly guessing the missing
letters before you (represented by the stick figure
in the gallows) are hanged. First, pick a letter and
scratch off the silver circle beneath it. If that letter
is correct, one or more numbers will tell you which
blanks you should write that letter in. But if you
guess incorrectly, a bold ✖ will be revealed, which
means you must draw in one of the stick figure's body
parts. (You can draw them in any order; the hangman
is generous that way.)

The stick figure's body has six parts: a head, a torso,
two arms, and two legs. If you spell the entire word or
phrase before the stick figure is completed, you win! If
you don't . . . well, it was nice knowing you. And now,
if you're ready, you may turn the page and begin.

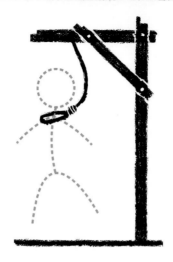

A B C D E F G

H I J K L M

N O P Q R S T

U V W X Y Z

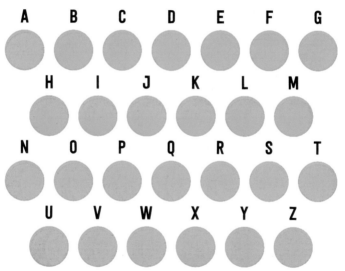

$\overline{}\ \overline{}\ \overline{}\ \overline{}\ \overline{}\qquad\overline{}\ \overline{}\ \overline{}\ \overline{}$

1 2 3 4 5   6 7 8 9

$\overline{}\ \overline{}\ \overline{}\ \overline{}\ \overline{}\ \overline{}$

10 11 12 13 14 15

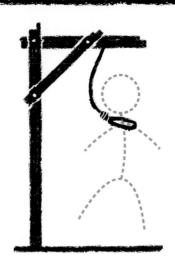

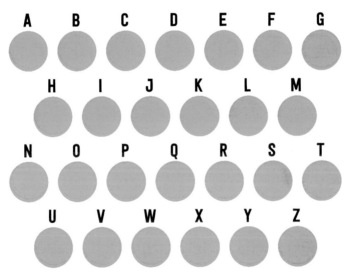

$\overline{}_{1}\ \overline{}_{2}\ \overline{}_{3}\ \overline{}_{4}\ \overline{}_{5}\ \overline{}_{6}\qquad\overline{}_{7}\ \overline{}_{8}\ \overline{}_{9}$

$\overline{}_{10}\ \overline{}_{11}\ \overline{}_{12}\qquad\overline{}_{13}\ \overline{}_{14}\ \overline{}_{15}\ \overline{}_{16}\ \overline{}_{17}$

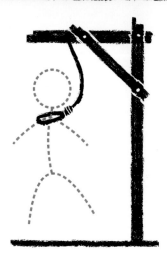

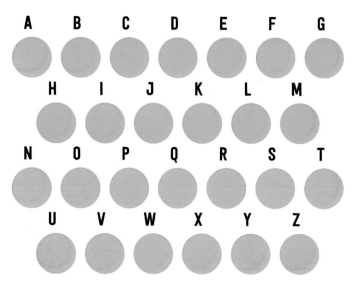

A B C D E F G

H I J K L M

N O P Q R S T

U V W X Y Z

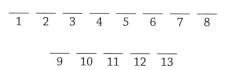

$\overline{}$ $\overline{}$ $\overline{}$ $\overline{}$ $\overline{}$ $\overline{}$ $\overline{}$ $\overline{}$
1 2 3 4 5 6 7 8

$\overline{}$ $\overline{}$ $\overline{}$ $\overline{}$ $\overline{}$
9 10 11 12 13

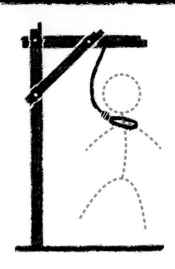

A B C D E F G

H I J K L M

N O P Q R S T

U V W X Y Z

$$\overline{}\ \overline{}\ \overline{}\ \overline{}\ \overline{}\ \overline{}\ \overline{}\ \overline{}\ \overline{}\ \overline{}$$
1 2 3 4 5 6 7 8 9 10

$$\overline{}\ \overline{}\ \overline{}\ \overline{}\ \overline{}\ \overline{}$$
11 12 13 14 15 16

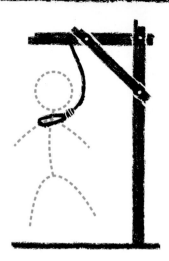

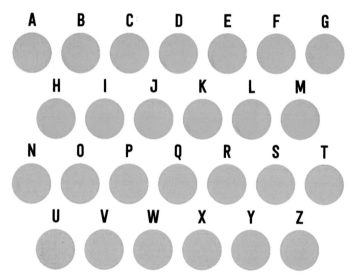

A B C D E F G

H I J K L M

N O P Q R S T

U V W X Y Z

$\overline{}$ $\overline{}$ $\overline{}$ $\overline{}$ $\quad$ $\overline{}$ $\overline{}$ $\overline{}$
1 2 3 4 5 6 7

$\overline{}$ $\overline{}$ $\overline{}$ $\overline{}$ $\overline{}$
8 9 10 11 12

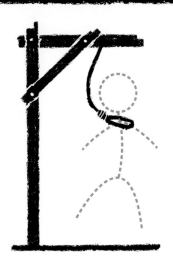

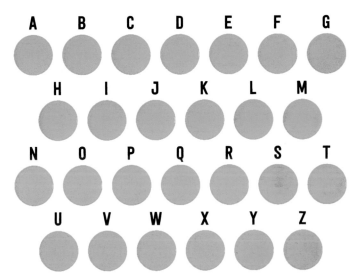

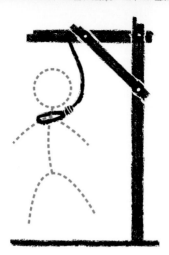

A B C D E F G

H I J K L M

N O P Q R S T

U V W X Y Z

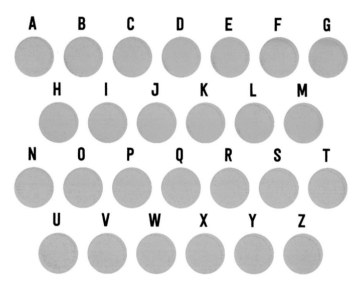

$\overline{\quad}$ $\overline{\quad}$ $\overline{\quad}$ $\overline{\quad}$ $\overline{\quad}$ $\overline{\quad}$ $\overline{\quad}$
1   2   3   4   5   6   7

$\overline{\quad}$ $\overline{\quad}$ $\overline{\quad}$ $\overline{\quad}$ $\overline{\quad}$ $\overline{\quad}$ $\overline{\quad}$
8   9   10   11   12   13   14

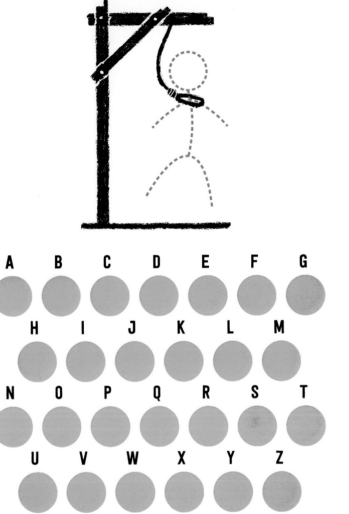

A   B   C   D   E   F   G

H   I   J   K   L   M

N   O   P   Q   R   S   T

U   V   W   X   Y   Z

 1   2   3   4   5   6   7   8   9   10   11   12

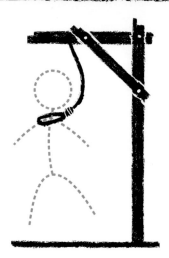

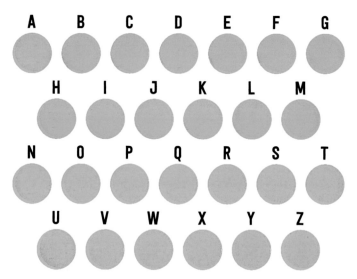

A   B   C   D   E   F   G

H   I   J   K   L   M

N   O   P   Q   R   S   T

U   V   W   X   Y   Z

‾‾ ‾‾ ‾‾ ‾‾ ‾‾ ‾‾
1   2   3   4   5   6

‾‾ ‾‾ ‾‾ ‾‾ ‾‾ ‾‾ ‾‾ ‾‾ ‾‾
7   8   9   10 11 12 13 14 15

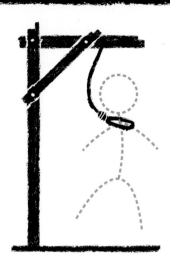

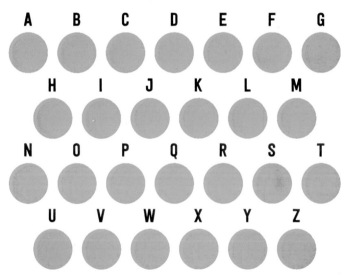

$\overline{}_{1}\ \overline{}_{2}\ \overline{}_{3}\ \overline{}_{4}\ \overline{}_{5}\ \overline{}_{6}\ \overline{}_{7}$

$\overline{}_{8}\ \overline{}_{9}\ \overline{}_{10}\ \overline{}_{11}\ \overline{}_{12}\ \overline{}_{13}$

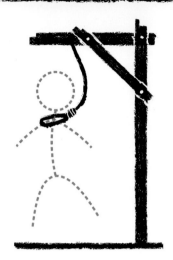

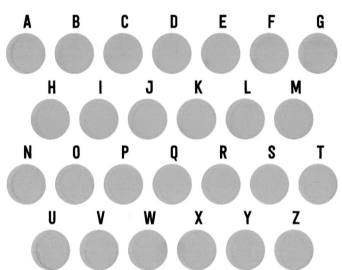

$\overline{}$ $\overline{}$ $\overline{}$ $\overline{}$ $\overline{}$ $\overline{}$ $\overline{}$ $\overline{}$ $\overline{}$ $\overline{}$ $\overline{}$ $\overline{}$
1   2   3   4   5   6   7   8   9   10   11   12

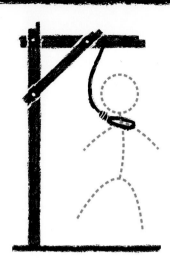

A B C D E F G

H I J K L M

N O P Q R S T

U V W X Y Z

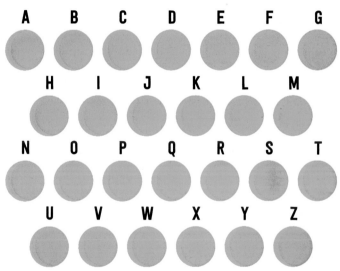

$\overline{}_{1}$ $\overline{}_{2}$ $\overline{}_{3}$ $\overline{}_{4}$ $^{-}$ $\overline{}_{5}$ $\overline{}_{6}$ $\overline{}_{7}$ $\overline{}_{8}$

$\overline{}_{9}$ $\overline{}_{10}$ $\overline{}_{11}$ $\overline{}_{12}$ $\overline{}_{13}$

15

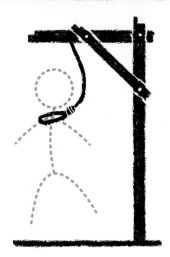

A B C D E F G

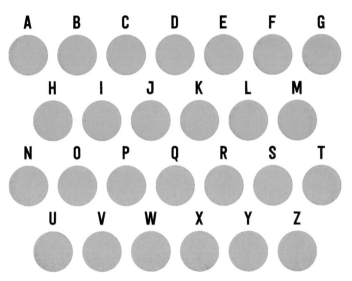

H I J K L M

N O P Q R S T

U V W X Y Z

$\overline{}_{1} \overline{}_{2} \overline{}_{3} \overline{}_{4} \overline{}_{5},$ $\overline{}_{6} \overline{}_{7} \overline{}_{8} \overline{}_{9} \overline{}_{10}$

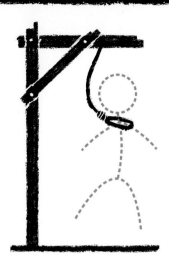

A B C D E F G

H I J K L M

N O P Q R S T

U V W X Y Z

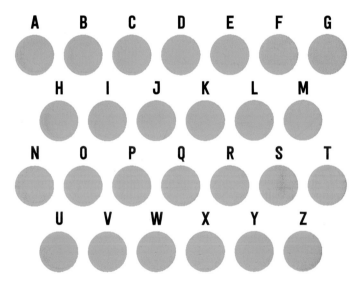

$\overline{}$ $\overline{}$ $\overline{}$ $\overline{}$ $\overline{}$
1 2 3 4 5

$\overline{}$ $\overline{}$ $\overline{}$ $\overline{}$ $\overline{}$ $\overline{}$ $\overline{}$ $\overline{}$ $\overline{}$
6 7 8 9 10 11 12 13 14

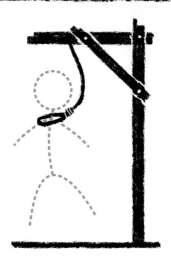

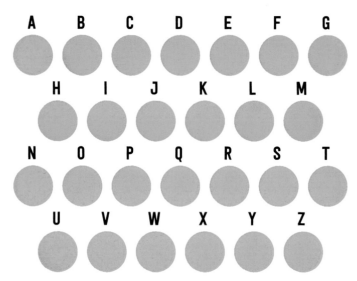

$$\overline{}_{1} \ \overline{}_{2} \ \overline{}_{3} \ \overline{}_{4} \ \overline{}_{5} \ \overline{}_{6}$$

$$\overline{}_{7} \ \overline{}_{8} \ \overline{}_{9} \ \overline{}_{10} \ \overline{}_{11} \ \overline{}_{12} \ \overline{}_{13}$$

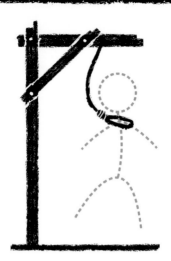

A B C D E F G

H I J K L M

N O P Q R S T

U V W X Y Z

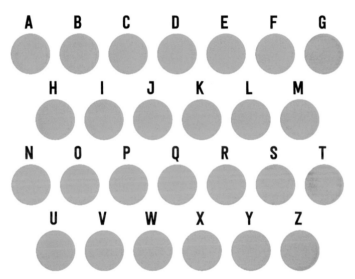

"
‾‾ ‾‾ ‾‾   ‾‾ ‾‾ ‾‾ ‾‾
1 2 3   4 5 6 7

"
‾‾ ‾‾ ‾‾ ‾‾
8 9 10 11

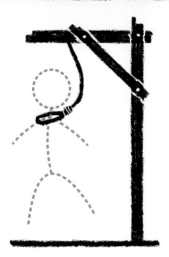

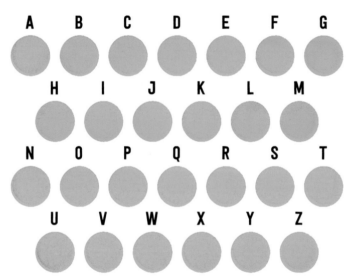

A   B   C   D   E   F   G

H   I   J   K   L   M

N   O   P   Q   R   S   T

U   V   W   X   Y   Z

___ ___ ___ ___ ___ ___ ___   ___ ___ ___ ___ ___
 1   2   3   4   5   6   7   8   9 10 11 12

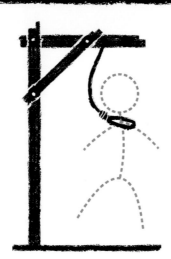

A   B   C   D   E   F   G

H   I   J   K   L   M

N   O   P   Q   R   S   T

U   V   W   X   Y   Z

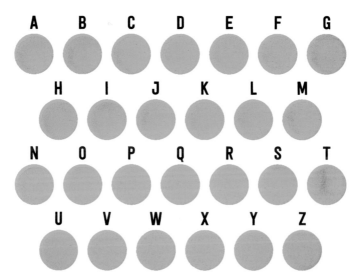

$$\overline{}_{1}\ \overline{}_{2}\ \overline{}_{3}\ \overline{}_{4}\qquad \overline{}_{5}\ \overline{}_{6}$$

$$\overline{}_{7}\ \overline{}_{8}\ \overline{}_{9}\ \overline{}_{10}\ \overline{}_{11}\ \overline{}_{12}\ \overline{}_{13}\ \overline{}_{14}$$

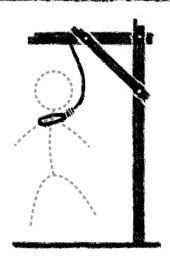

A **B** **C** **D** **E** **F** **G**

H **I** **J** **K** **L** **M**

N **O** **P** **Q** **R** **S** **T**

U **V** **W** **X** **Y** **Z**

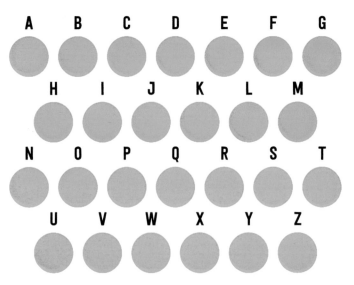

$$\overline{}_{1} \quad \overline{}_{2} \quad \overline{}_{3} \quad \overline{}_{4} \quad \overline{}_{5} \quad \overline{}_{6} \quad \overline{}_{7}$$

$$\overline{}_{8} \quad \overline{}_{9} \quad \overline{}_{10} \quad \overline{}_{11} \quad \overline{}_{12} \quad \overline{}_{13} \quad \overline{}_{14} \quad \overline{}_{15}$$

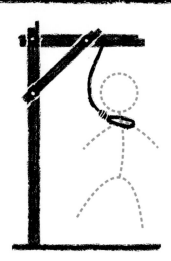

A B C D E F G

H I J K L M

N O P Q R S T

U V W X Y Z

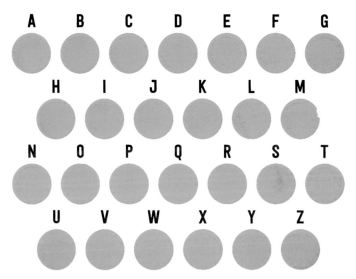

$\overline{}$ $\overline{}$ $\overline{}$ $\overline{}$ $\overline{}$ $\overline{}$ $\overline{}$ $\overline{}$ $\overline{}$ $\overline{}$ $\overline{}$
1 2 3 4 5 6 7   8 9 10 11

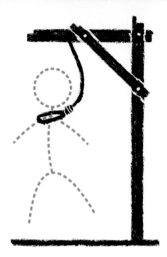

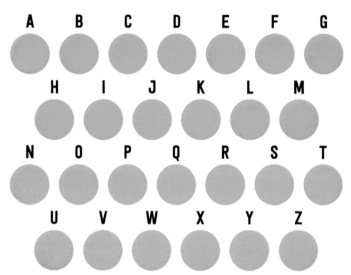

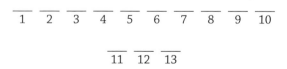

$$\overline{}_{1} \ \overline{}_{2} \ \overline{}_{3} \ \overline{}_{4} \ \overline{}_{5} \ \overline{}_{6} \ \overline{}_{7} \ \overline{}_{8} \ \overline{}_{9} \ \overline{}_{10} \ ,$$

$$\overline{}_{11} \ \overline{}_{12} \ \overline{}_{13}$$

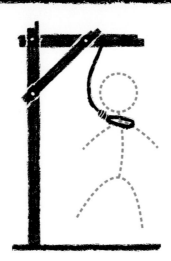

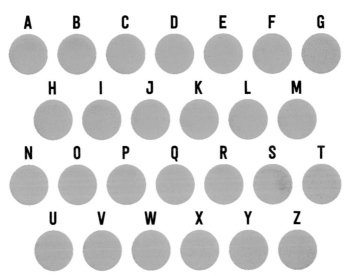

A B C D E F G

H I J K L M

N O P Q R S T

U V W X Y Z

__ __ __ __ __ __   __ __ __ __ __ __
1   2   3   4   5   6   7   8   9   10 11 12

25

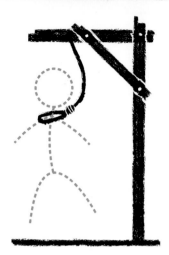

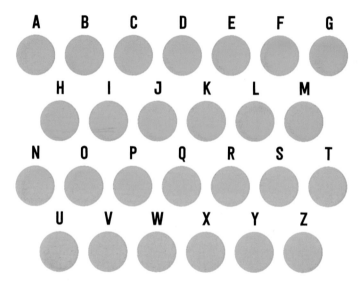

$\overline{\rule{1em}{0pt}}$ $\overline{\rule{1em}{0pt}}$ $\overline{\rule{1em}{0pt}}$ $\overline{\rule{1em}{0pt}}$ $\overline{\rule{1em}{0pt}}$ $\overline{\rule{1em}{0pt}}$ $\overline{\rule{1em}{0pt}}$ $\overline{\rule{1em}{0pt}}$ $\overline{\rule{1em}{0pt}}$ $\overline{\rule{1em}{0pt}}$ $\overline{\rule{1em}{0pt}}$
1 2 3 4 5 6 7 8 9 10 11

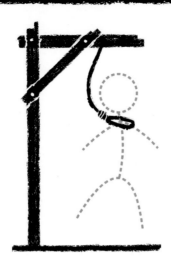

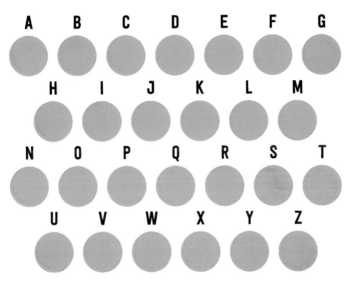

| A | B | C | D | E | F | G |

| H | I | J | K | L | M |

| N | O | P | Q | R | S | T |

| U | V | W | X | Y | Z |

___ ___ ___ ___ ___ ___ ___
 1   2   3   4   5   6   7

___ ___ ___ ___ ___ ___
 8   9 10 11 12 13

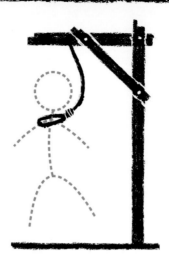

A B C D E F G

H I J K L M

N O P Q R S T

U V W X Y Z

$\overline{}_{1}$ $\overline{}_{2}$ $\overline{}_{3}$ $\overline{}_{4}$ $\overline{}_{5}$ $\overline{}_{6}$ $\overline{}_{7}$ $\overline{}_{8}$ $\overline{}_{9}$

$\overline{}_{10}$ $\overline{}_{11}$ $\overline{}_{12}$ $\overline{}_{13}$

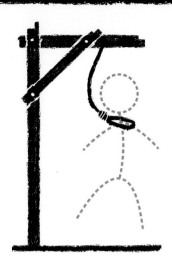

A B C D E F G

H I J K L M

N O P Q R S T

U V W X Y Z

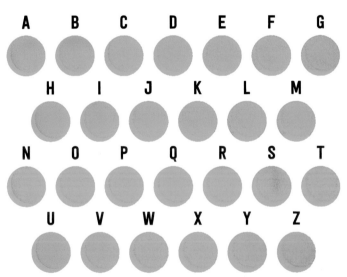

$\overline{}\ \overline{}\ \overline{}\ \overline{}\ \overline{}\ \overline{}\ \overline{}$
1   2   3   4   5   6   7

$\overline{}\ \overline{}\ \overline{}\ \overline{}\ \overline{}\ \overline{}$
8   9   10   11   12   13

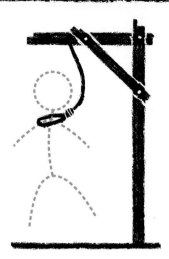

A B C D E F G

H I J K L M

N O P Q R S T

U V W X Y Z

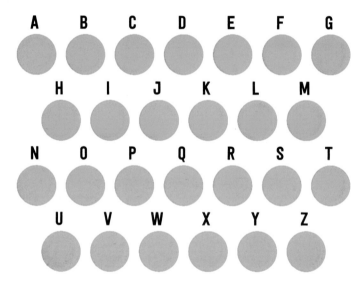

$\overline{}_{1}$ $\overline{}_{2}$ $\overline{}_{3}$ $\overline{}_{4}$ $\overline{}_{5}$ $\overline{}_{6}$ $\overline{}_{7}$ $\overline{}_{8}$ $\overline{}_{9}$

$\overline{}_{10}$ $\overline{}_{11}$ $\overline{}_{12}$ $\overline{}_{13}$

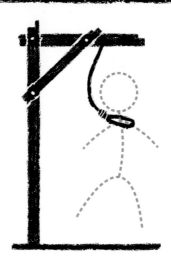

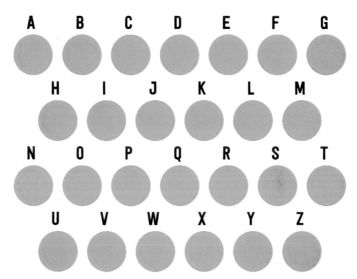

A B C D E F G

H I J K L M

N O P Q R S T

U V W X Y Z

$\overline{}_{1}\ \overline{}_{2}\ \overline{}_{3}\ \overline{}_{4}\ \overline{}_{5}\ \overline{}_{6}\ -\ \overline{}_{7}\ \overline{}_{8}\ -\ \overline{}_{9}\ \overline{}_{10}\ \overline{}_{11}$

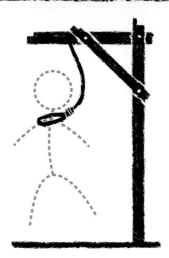

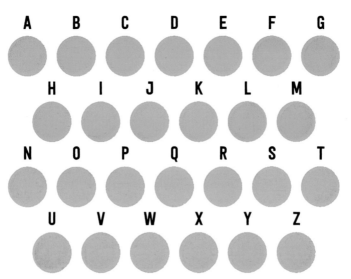

$\overline{}$ $\overline{}$ $\overline{}$ $\overline{}$ $\overline{}$ $\overline{}$ $\overline{}$ $\overline{}$
1   2   3   4   5   6   7   8

$\overline{}$ $\overline{}$ $\overline{}$ $\overline{}$ $\overline{}$ $\overline{}$ $\overline{}$
9 10 11 12 13 14 15

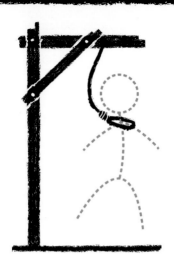

A	B	C	D	E	F	G
○	○	○	○	○	○	○

H	I	J	K	L	M
○	○	○	○	○	○

N	O	P	Q	R	S	T
○	○	○	○	○	○	○

U	V	W	X	Y	Z
○	○	○	○	○	○

$\overline{}_{1}\ \overline{}_{2}\ \overline{}_{3}\quad \overline{}_{4}\ \overline{}_{5}\ \overline{}_{6}\ \overline{}_{7}\ \overline{}_{8}\ \overline{}_{9}$

$\overline{}_{10}\ \overline{}_{11}\ \overline{}_{12}\ \overline{}_{13}\ \overline{}_{14}\ \overline{}_{15}\ \overline{}_{16}$

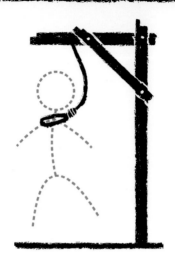

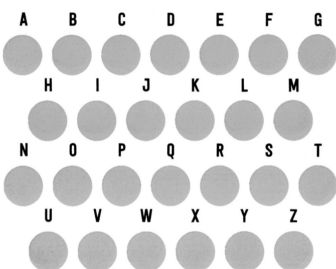

$\overline{}$ $\overline{}$ $\overline{}$ $\overline{}$ $\overline{}$ $\overline{}$ $\overline{}$ $\overline{}$ $\overline{}$
1   2   3   4   5   6   7   8   9

A ○ **B** ○ **C** ○ **D** ○ **E** ○ **F** ○ **G** ○

H ○ **I** ○ **J** ○ **K** ○ **L** ○ **M** ○

N ○ **O** ○ **P** ○ **Q** ○ **R** ○ **S** ○ **T** ○

U ○ **V** ○ **W** ○ **X** ○ **Y** ○ **Z** ○

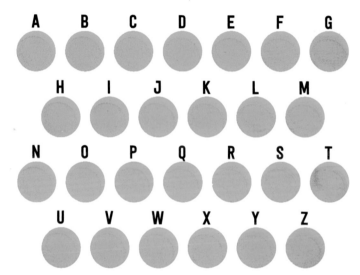

$$\overline{}_1 \ \overline{}_2 \ \overline{}_3 \ \overline{}_4 \ \overline{}_5 \ \overline{}_6$$

$$\overline{}_7 \ \overline{}_8 \ \overline{}_9 \ \overline{}_{10} \ \overline{}_{11} \ \overline{}_{12} \ \overline{}_{13} \ \overline{}_{14}$$

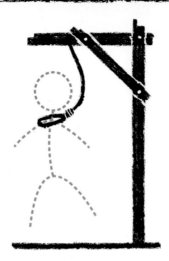

A B C D E F G

H I J K L M

N O P Q R S T

U V W X Y Z

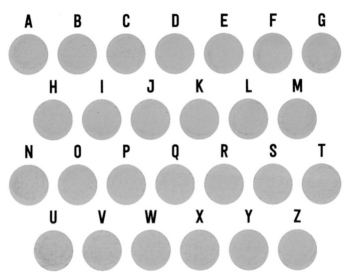

___ ___ ___ ___ ___ ___ ___
 1   2   3   4   5   6   7

___ ___ ___ ___ ___ ___ ___ ___ ___
 8   9 10 11 12 13 14 15 16

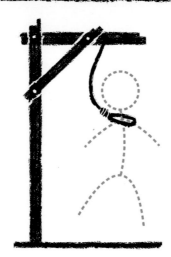

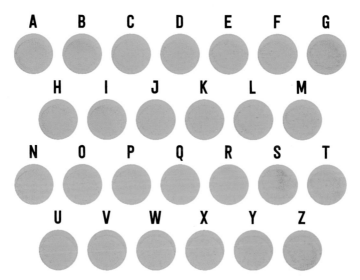

$$\underline{}_{1} \ \underline{}_{2} \ \underline{}_{3} \ \underline{}_{4} \ \underline{}_{5} \qquad \underline{}_{6} \ \underline{}_{7} \ \underline{}_{8} \ \underline{}_{9}$$

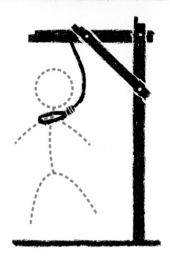

| A | B | C | D | E | F | G |

| H | I | J | K | L | M |

| N | O | P | Q | R | S | T |

| U | V | W | X | Y | Z |

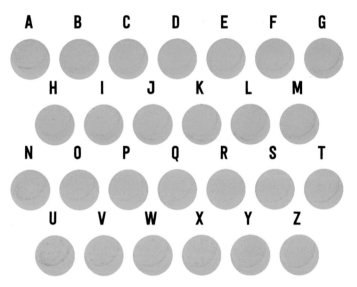

$\overline{}_{1}$ $\overline{}_{2}$ $\overline{}_{3}$ $\overline{}_{4}$ $\quad$ $\overline{}_{5}$ $\overline{}_{6}$ $\overline{}_{7}$ $\overline{}_{8}$ $\overline{}_{9}$

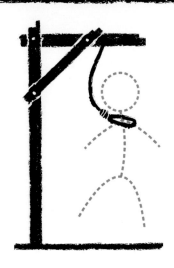

A B C D E F G

H I J K L M

N O P Q R S T

U V W X Y Z

___ ___ ___ ___ ___ ___ ___ ___
1   2   3   4   5   6   7   8

___ ___ ___ ___ ___
9 10 11 12 13

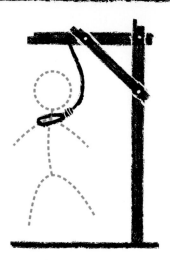

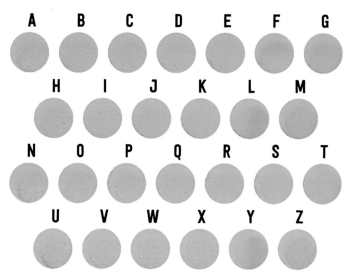

A B C D E F G

H I J K L M

N O P Q R S T

U V W X Y Z

—————————— ——————————
1 2 3 4 5 6 7   8 9 10 11

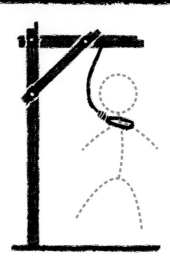

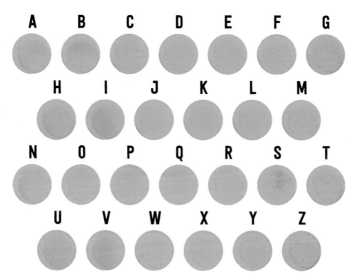

$$\overline{\quad}_{1} \ \overline{\quad}_{2} \ \overline{\quad}_{3} \ \overline{\quad}_{4} \ \overline{\quad}_{5} \ \overline{\quad}_{6}$$

$$\overline{\quad}_{7} \ \overline{\quad}_{8} \ \overline{\quad}_{9} \ \overline{\quad}_{10} \ \overline{\quad}_{11} \ \overline{\quad}_{12} \ \overline{\quad}_{13} \ \overline{\quad}_{14}$$

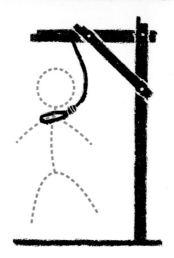

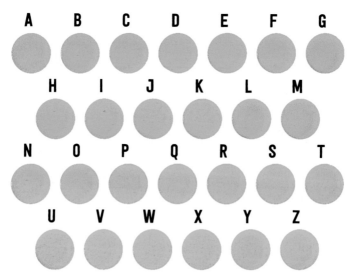

$$\overline{}_{1} \quad \overline{}_{2} \quad \overline{}_{3} \qquad \overline{}_{4} \quad \overline{}_{5} \quad \overline{}_{6} \quad \overline{}_{7} \quad \overline{}_{8} \quad \overline{}_{9}$$

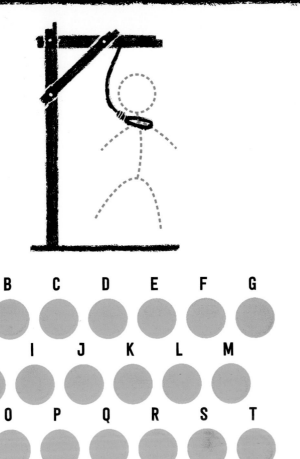

A B C D E F G

H I J K L M

N O P Q R S T

U V W X Y Z

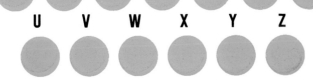

—— —— —— —— —— —— —— —— —— —— ——
1 2 3 4 5 6 7 8   9 10 11

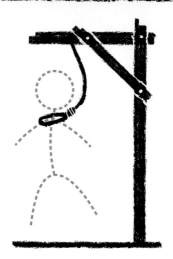

A B C D E F G

H I J K L M

N O P Q R S T

U V W X Y Z

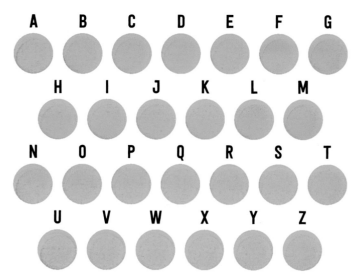

$\overline{\ \ }$ $\overline{\ \ }$ $\overline{\ \ }$ $\overline{\ \ }$ $\overline{\ \ }$ $\overline{\ \ }$ $\overline{\ \ }$ $\overline{\ \ }$
1   2   3   4   5   6   7   8

$\overline{\ \ }$ $\overline{\ \ }$ $\overline{\ \ }$ $\overline{\ \ }$ $\overline{\ \ }$ $\overline{\ \ }$
9   10 11 12 13 14

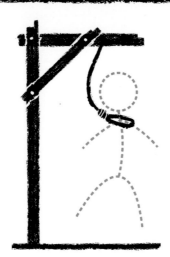

A B C D E F G

H I J K L M

N O P Q R S T

U V W X Y Z

‾ ‾ ‾ ‾ ‾ ‾ ‾ ‾ ‾ ‾
1 2 3 4 5 6 7 8 9 10

45

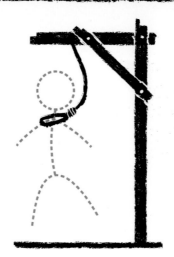

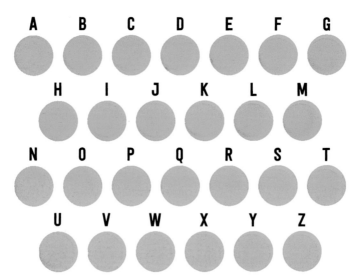

$\overline{}$ $\overline{}$ $\overline{}$ $\overline{}$ $\overline{}$ $\overline{}$ $\overline{}$ $\overline{}$ $\overline{}$
1   2   3   4   5   6   7   8   9

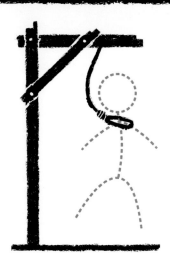

A B C D E F G

H I J K L M

N O P Q R S T

U V W X Y Z

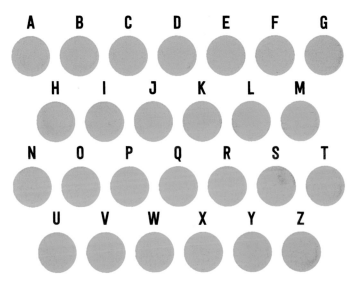

$\overline{}$ $\overline{}$ $\overline{}$ $\overline{}$ $\overline{}$ $\overline{}$ $\overline{}$ $\overline{}$ $\overline{}$ $\overline{}$ $\overline{}$
1   2   3   4   5   6   7   8   9   10   11

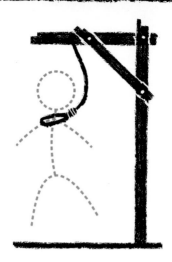

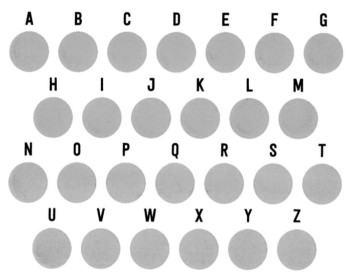

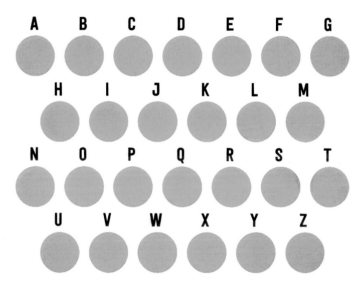

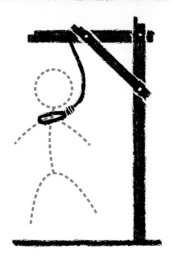

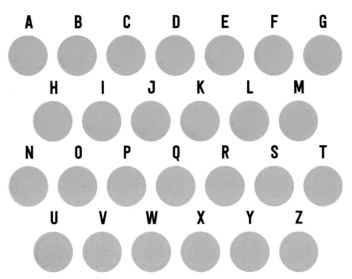

$\overline{}$ $\overline{}$ $\overline{}$ $\overline{}$ $\overline{}$ $\quad$ $\overline{}$ $\overline{}$ $\overline{}$ $\overline{}$ $\overline{}$
1 $\quad$ 2 $\quad$ 3 $\quad$ 4 $\quad$ 5 $\qquad$ 6 $\quad$ 7 $\quad$ 8 $\quad$ 9 $\quad$ 10

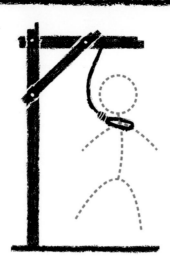

A B C D E F G

H I J K L M

N O P Q R S T

U V W X Y Z

$$\overline{}_{1}\ \overline{}_{2}\ \overline{}_{3}\ \overline{}_{4}\ \overline{}_{5}\qquad\overline{}_{6}\ \overline{}_{7}\ \overline{}_{8}\ \overline{}_{9}\ \overline{}_{10}$$

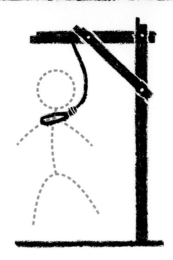

A B C D E F G

H I J K L M

N O P Q R S T

U V W X Y Z

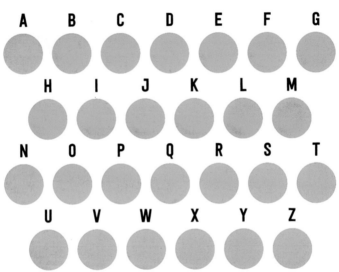

$\overline{}$ $\overline{}$ $\overline{}$ $\overline{}$ $\overline{}$ $\overline{}$ $\overline{}$ $\overline{}$ $\overline{}$ $\overline{}$
1 2 3 4 5 6 7 8 9 10

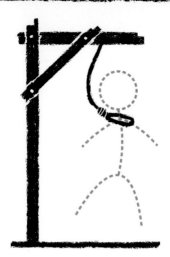

A B C D E F G

H I J K L M

N O P Q R S T

U V W X Y Z

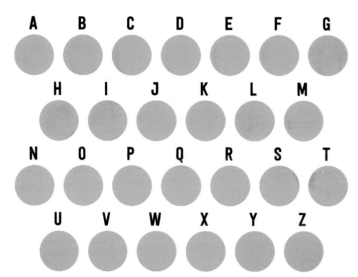

—— —— —— —— ——   —— —— —— —— —— —— ——
1   2   3   4   5   6   7   8   9   10   11   12

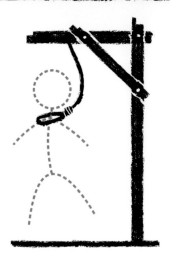

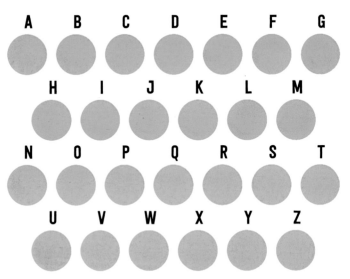

A B C D E F G

H I J K L M

N O P Q R S T

U V W X Y Z

$\overline{}_{1}$ $\overline{}_{2}$ $\overline{}_{3}$ $\overline{}_{4}$ $\overline{}_{5}$ $\overline{}_{6}$ $\overline{}_{7}$ $\overline{}_{8}$ $\overline{}_{9}$ $\overline{}_{10}$ $\overline{}_{11}$

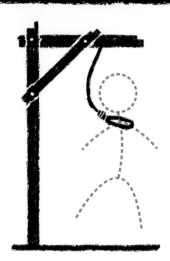

A ● **B** ● **C** ● **D** ● **E** ● **F** ● **G** ●

H ● **I** ● **J** ● **K** ● **L** ● **M** ●

N ● **O** ● **P** ● **Q** ● **R** ● **S** ● **T** ●

U ● **V** ● **W** ● **X** ● **Y** ● **Z** ●

$$\overline{}_{1}\ \overline{}_{2}\ \overline{}_{3}\ \overline{}_{4}\ -\ \overline{}_{5}$$

$$\overline{}_{6}\ \overline{}_{7}\ \overline{}_{8}\ \overline{}_{9}\ \overline{}_{10}\ \overline{}_{11}\ -\ \overline{}_{12}\ \overline{}_{13}\ \overline{}_{14}$$

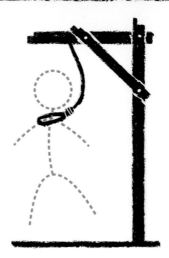

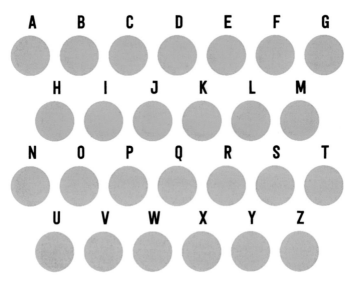

$$\overline{}_{1} \ \overline{}_{2} \ \overline{}_{3} \ \overline{}_{4} \ \overline{}_{5} \ \overline{}_{6}$$

$$\overline{}_{7} \ \overline{}_{8} \ \overline{}_{9} \ \overline{}_{10} \ \overline{}_{11} \ \overline{}_{12} \ \overline{}_{13}$$

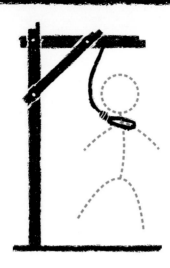

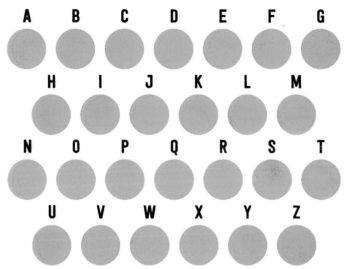

A B C D E F G

H I J K L M

N O P Q R S T

U V W X Y Z

$\overline{}_{1}\ \overline{}_{2}\ \overline{}_{3}\ \overline{}_{4}\qquad \overline{}_{5}\ \overline{}_{6}\ \overline{}_{7}\ \overline{}_{8}\ \overline{}_{9}\ \overline{}_{10}\ \overline{}_{11}\ \overline{}_{12}$

57

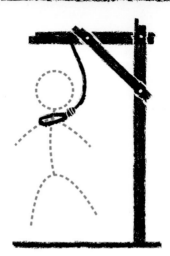

A B C D E F G

H I J K L M

N O P Q R S T

U V W X Y Z

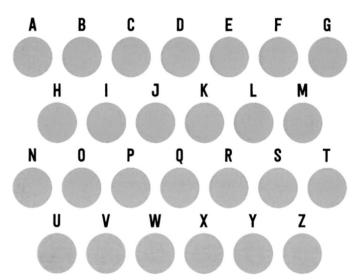

‾‾ ‾‾ ‾‾ ‾‾ ‾‾ ‾‾ ‾‾
1 2 3 4 5 6 7

‾‾ ‾‾ ‾‾ ‾‾ ‾‾ ‾‾ ‾‾
8 9 10 11 12 13 14

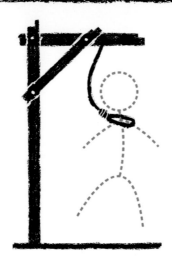

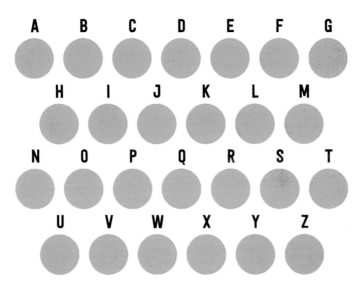

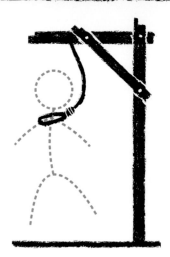

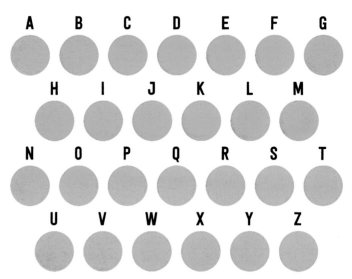

| A | B | C | D | E | F | G |

| H | I | J | K | L | M |

| N | O | P | Q | R | S | T |

| U | V | W | X | Y | Z |

$\overline{\quad}$ $\overline{\quad}$ $\overline{\quad}$ $\overline{\quad}$ $\overline{\quad}$ $\overline{\quad}$ $\overline{\quad}$ $\overline{\quad}$ $\overline{\quad}$ $\overline{\quad}$
1   2   3   4   5   6   7   8   9   10

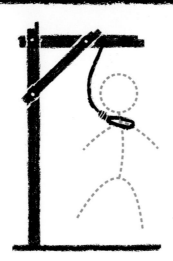

A B C D E F G

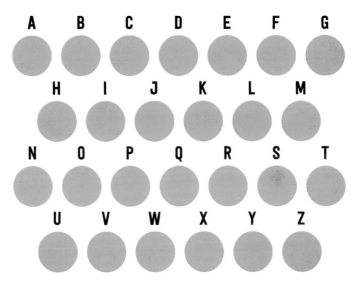

H I J K L M

N O P Q R S T

U V W X Y Z

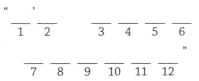

" $\overline{}$, $\overline{}$
$\overline{1}$ $\overline{2}$ $\overline{3}$ $\overline{4}$ $\overline{5}$ $\overline{6}$

"
$\overline{7}$ $\overline{8}$ $\overline{9}$ $\overline{10}$ $\overline{11}$ $\overline{12}$

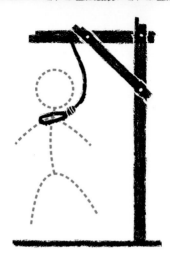

A B C D E F G

H I J K L M

N O P Q R S T

U V W X Y Z

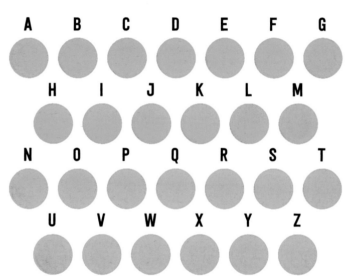

$\overline{}_{1}$ $\overline{}_{2}$ $\overline{}_{3}$ $\overline{}_{4}$ $\overline{}_{5}$ $\overline{}_{6}$ $\overline{}_{7}$ $\overline{}_{8}$ $\overline{}_{9}$

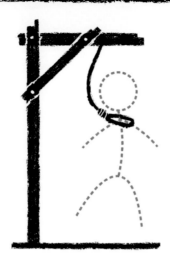

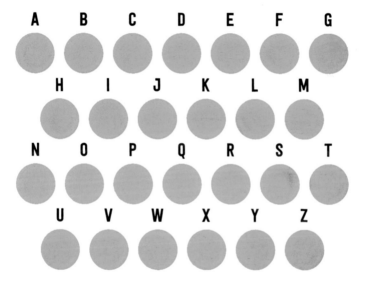

A   B   C   D   E   F   G

H   I   J   K   L   M

N   O   P   Q   R   S   T

U   V   W   X   Y   Z

___ ___ ___ ___ ___   ___ ___ ___ ___ ___ ___
1 2 3 4 5   6 7 8 9 10 11

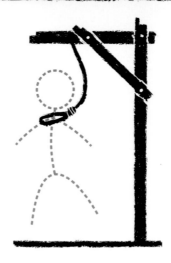

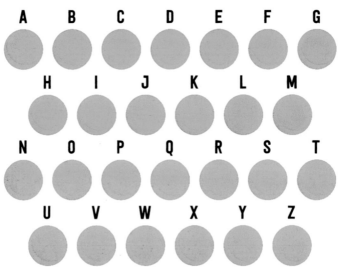

$$\overline{\quad}\ \overline{\quad}\ \overline{\quad}\ \overline{\quad}\ \overline{\quad}\ \overline{\quad}\ \overline{\quad}\ \overline{\quad}\ \overline{\quad}\ \overline{\quad}$$
1 2 3 4 5 6 7 8 9 10

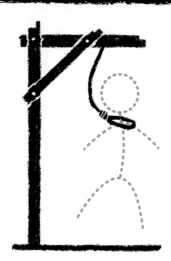

A B C D E F G

H I J K L M

N O P Q R S T

U V W X Y Z

$\overline{\quad}_{1}$ $\overline{\quad}_{2}$ $\overline{\quad}_{3}$ $\overline{\quad}_{4}$ $\overline{\quad}_{5}$ $\overline{\quad}_{6}$ $\overline{\quad}_{7}$

$\overline{\quad}_{8}$ $\overline{\quad}_{9}$ $\overline{\quad}_{10}$ $\overline{\quad}_{11}$ $\overline{\quad}_{12}$ $\overline{\quad}_{13}$ $\overline{\quad}_{14}$

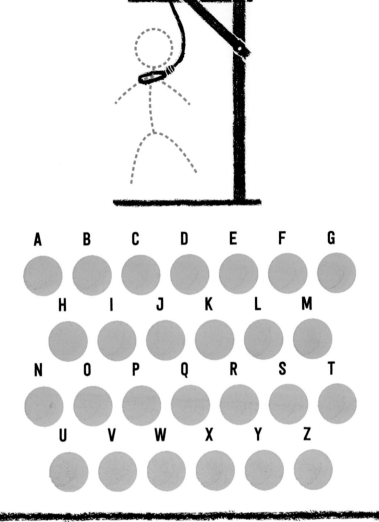

A   B   C   D   E   F   G

H   I   J   K   L   M

N   O   P   Q   R   S   T

U   V   W   X   Y   Z

$\overline{\quad}_1 \overline{\quad}_2 \overline{\quad}_3 \overline{\quad}_4 \overline{\quad}_5 \overline{\quad}_6 \overline{\quad}_7$, $\overline{\quad}_8 \overline{\quad}_9 \overline{\quad}_{10} \overline{\quad}_{11} \overline{\quad}_{12}$

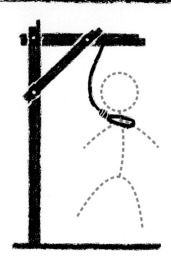

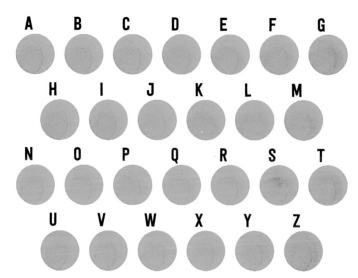

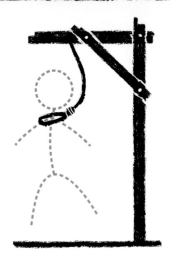

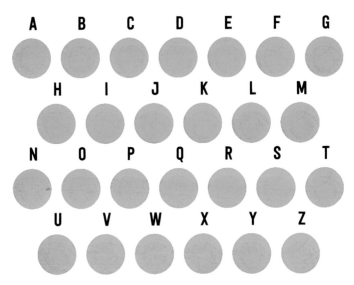

A   B   C   D   E   F   G

H   I   J   K   L   M

N   O   P   Q   R   S   T

U   V   W   X   Y   Z

$\overline{}_{1}$ $\overline{}_{2}$ $\overline{}_{3}$ $\overline{}_{4}$ $\overline{}_{5}$ $\overline{}_{6}$ $\overline{}_{7}$ $\overline{}_{8}$ $\overline{}_{9}$ $\overline{}_{10}$ $\overline{}_{11}$

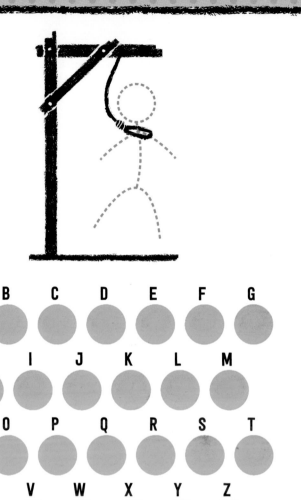

A B C D E F G

H I J K L M

N O P Q R S T

U V W X Y Z

$\overline{}_{1}$ $\overline{}_{2}$ $\overline{}_{3}$ $\overline{}_{4}$ $\overline{}_{5}$ $\overline{}_{6}$ $\overline{}_{7}$ $\overline{}_{8}$ $\overline{}_{9}$ $\overline{}_{10}$

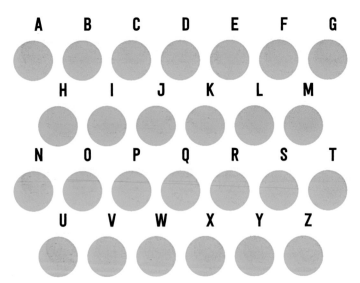

$$\overline{}\ \overline{}\ \overline{}\ \overline{}\qquad\overline{}\ \overline{}\ \overline{}\ \overline{}\ \overline{}$$

1 2 3 4   5 6 7 8 9

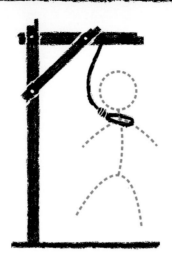

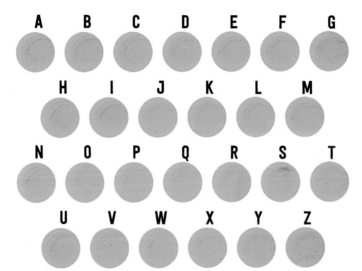

$\overline{}\ \overline{}\ \overline{}\ \overline{}\ \overline{}\ \overline{}$
1 2 3 4 5 6

$\overline{}\ \overline{}\ \overline{}\ \overline{}\ \overline{}\ \overline{}\ \overline{}\ \overline{}\ \overline{}$
7 8 9 10 11 12 13 14 15

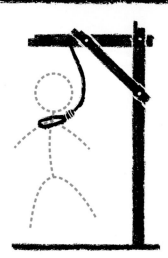

A B C D E F G

H I J K L M

N O P Q R S T

U V W X Y Z

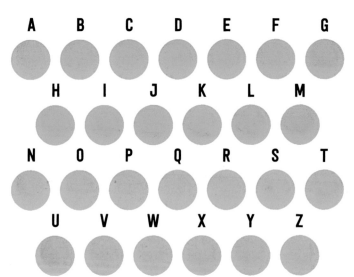

‾‾ ‾‾ ‾‾ ‾‾ ‾‾ ‾‾ ‾‾
1 2 3 4 5 6 7

‾‾ ‾‾ ‾‾ ‾‾ ‾‾ ‾‾ ‾‾ ‾‾ ‾‾
8 9 10 11 12 13 14 15 16

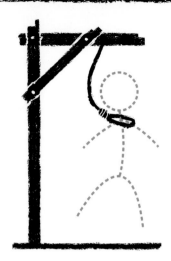

A B C D E F G

H I J K L M

N O P Q R S T

U V W X Y Z

___ ___ ___ ___ ___ ___ ___ ___ ___
1   2   3   4   5   6   7   8   9

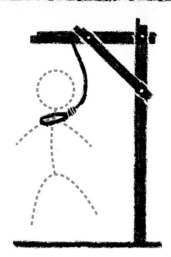

A B C D E F G

H I J K L M

N O P Q R S T

U V W X Y Z

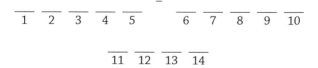

$$\overline{}_{1} \ \overline{}_{2} \ \overline{}_{3} \ \overline{}_{4} \ \overline{}_{5} \quad \overline{}_{6} \ \overline{}_{7} \ \overline{}_{8} \ \overline{}_{9} \ \overline{}_{10}$$

$$\overline{}_{11} \ \overline{}_{12} \ \overline{}_{13} \ \overline{}_{14}$$

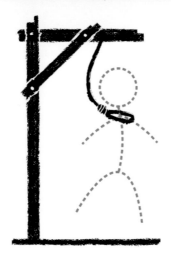

A B C D E F G

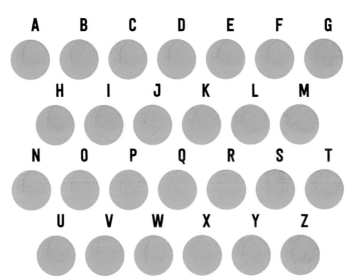

H I J K L M

N O P Q R S T

U V W X Y Z

$$\overline{}\ \overline{}\ \overline{}\qquad\overline{}\ \overline{}\ \overline{}\ \overline{}\ \overline{}\ \overline{}$$
1 2 3   4 5 6 7 8 9

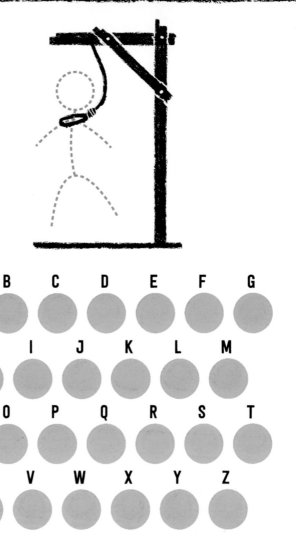

A B C D E F G

H I J K L M

N O P Q R S T

U V W X Y Z

$\overline{}$ $\overline{}$ $\overline{}$ $\overline{}$ $\overline{}$ $\overline{}$ $\overline{}$
1 2 3 4 5 6 7

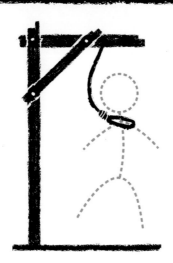

A ⬤ **B** ⬤ **C** ⬤ **D** ⬤ **E** ⬤ **F** ⬤ **G** ⬤

H ⬤ **I** ⬤ **J** ⬤ **K** ⬤ **L** ⬤ **M** ⬤

N ⬤ **O** ⬤ **P** ⬤ **Q** ⬤ **R** ⬤ **S** ⬤ **T** ⬤

U ⬤ **V** ⬤ **W** ⬤ **X** ⬤ **Y** ⬤ **Z** ⬤

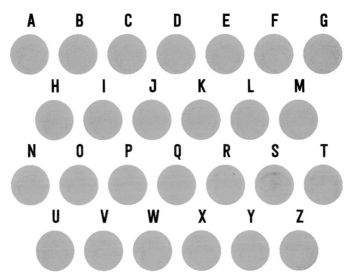

$\overline{}\ \overline{}\ \overline{}\ \overline{}\quad\overline{}\ \overline{}\ \overline{}\ \overline{}\ \overline{}\ \overline{}$
1   2   3   4   5   6   7   8   9   10

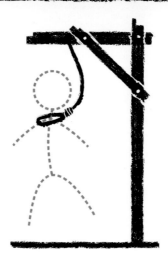

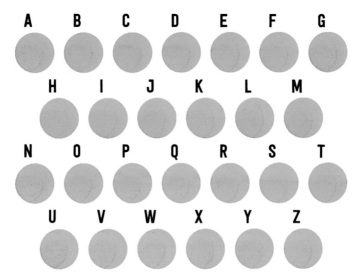

<u> </u> <u> </u> <u> </u>   <u> </u> <u> </u> <u> </u> <u> </u> <u> </u> <u> </u> <u> </u> <u> </u>
1 2 3   4 5 6 7 8 9 10 11

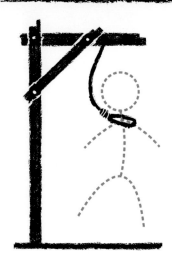

A B C D E F G

H I J K L M

N O P Q R S T

U V W X Y Z

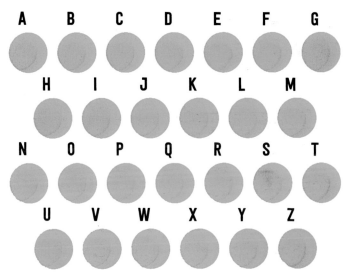

$\overline{}$ $\overline{}$ $\overline{}$ $\overline{}$ $\overline{}$ $\overline{}$ $\overline{}$ $\overline{}$
1 2 3 4 5 6 7 8

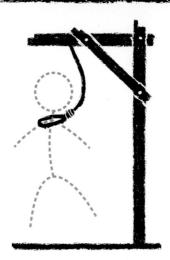

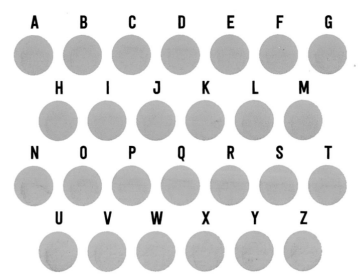

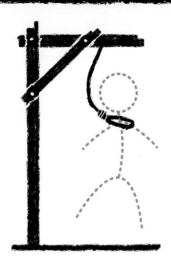

A B C D E F G

H I J K L M

N O P Q R S T

U V W X Y Z

$$\overline{}_{1} \overline{}_{2} \overline{}_{3} \overline{}_{4} \overline{}_{5} \quad \overline{}_{6} \overline{}_{7} \overline{}_{8} \overline{}_{9}$$

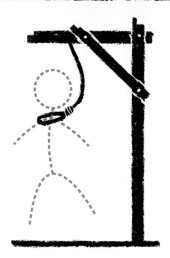

A B C D E F G

H I J K L M

N O P Q R S T

U V W X Y Z

$\overline{}$ $\overline{}$ $\overline{}$ $\overline{}$ $\overline{}$ $\overline{}$ $\qquad$ $\overline{}$ $\overline{}$ $\overline{}$ $\overline{}$ $\overline{}$
1   2   3   4   5   6   7   8   9   10   11

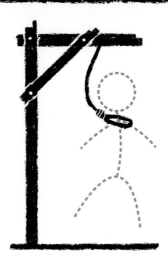

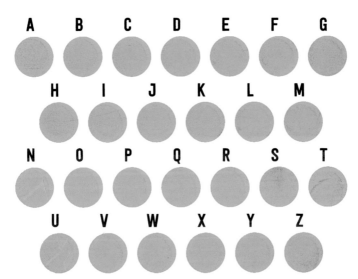

A B C D E F G

H I J K L M

N O P Q R S T

U V W X Y Z

___ ___ ___ ___   ___ ___ ___ ___ ___ ___
1   2   3   4   5   6   7   8   9   10

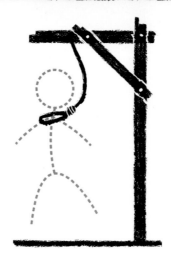

A B C D E F G

H I J K L M

N O P Q R S T

U V W X Y Z

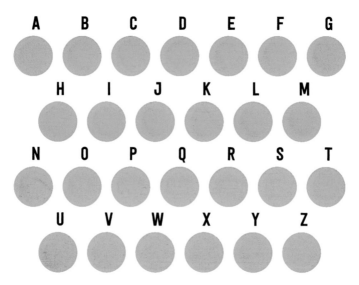

$$\overline{\quad}_1 \ \overline{\quad}_2 \ \overline{\quad}_3 \ \overline{\quad}_4 \ \overline{\quad}_5 \ \overline{\quad}_6 \ \overline{\quad}_7 \ \overline{\quad}_8 \ \overline{\quad}_9$$

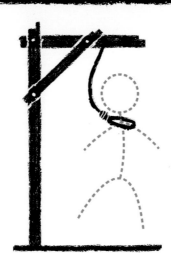

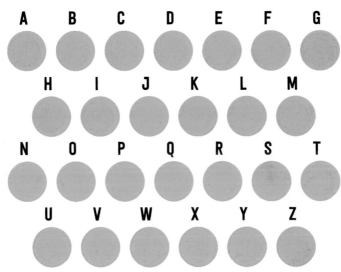

$$\overline{}\ \overline{}\ \overline{}\ \overline{}\ \overline{}\ \overline{}\ \overline{}\ \overline{}\ \overline{}\ \overline{}\ \overline{}$$
1   2   3   4   5   6   7   8   9   10   11

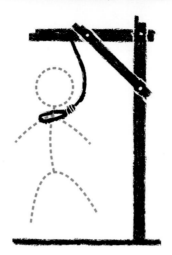

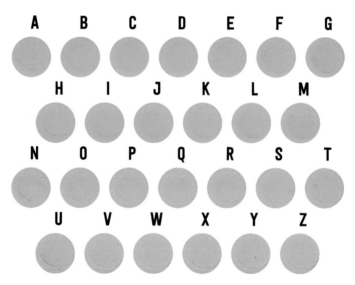

$\overline{}_{1}\ \overline{}_{2}\ \overline{}_{3}\ \overline{}_{4}\qquad \overline{}_{5}\ \overline{}_{6}\ \overline{}_{7}\ \overline{}_{8}\ \overline{}_{9}$

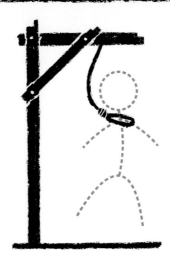

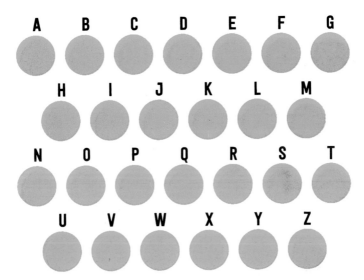

| A | B | C | D | E | F | G |

| H | I | J | K | L | M |

| N | O | P | Q | R | S | T |

| U | V | W | X | Y | Z |

‾1‾ ‾2‾ ‾3‾ ‾4‾ ‾5‾ ‾6‾ ‾7‾ ‾8‾ ‾9‾ ‾10‾ ‾11‾

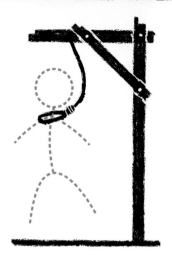

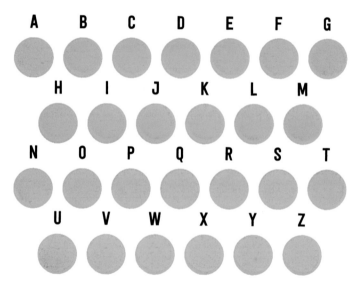

$\overline{}_{1}$ $\overline{}_{2}$ $\overline{}_{3}$ $\overline{}_{4}$ $\overline{}_{5}$ $\overline{}_{6}$ $\overline{}_{7}$ $\overline{}_{8}$ $\overline{}_{9}$ $\overline{}_{10}$

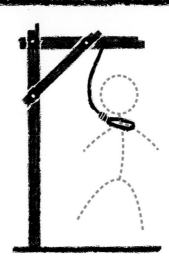

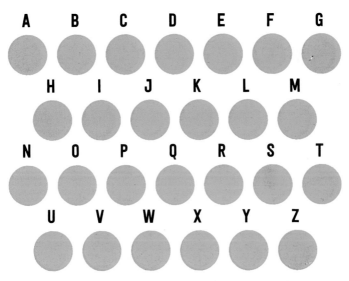

$\overline{}_{1} \overline{}_{2} \overline{}_{3} \overline{}_{4} \overline{}_{5} \overline{}_{6} \qquad \overline{}_{7} \overline{}_{8} \overline{}_{9} \overline{}_{10} \overline{}_{11}$

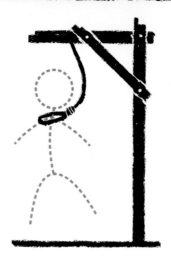

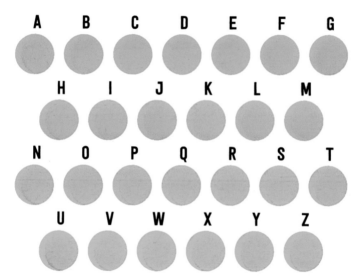

$\overline{}_{1}$ $\overline{}_{2}$ $\overline{}_{3}$ $\overline{}_{4}$ $\overline{}_{5}$ $\overline{}_{6}$ $\overline{}_{7}$ $\overline{}_{8}$ $\overline{}_{9}$ $\overline{}_{10}$ $\overline{}_{11}$ $\overline{}_{12}$

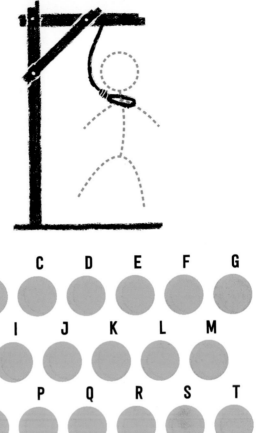

A   B   C   D   E   F   G

H   I   J   K   L   M

N   O   P   Q   R   S   T

U   V   W   X   Y   Z

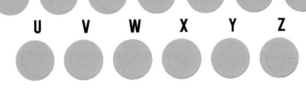

$\overline{}\ \overline{}\ \overline{}\ \overline{}\ \overline{}\ \overline{}\ \overline{}\ \overline{}$
1   2   3   4   5   6   7   8

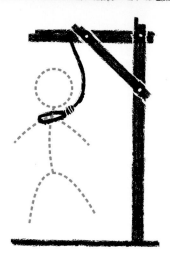

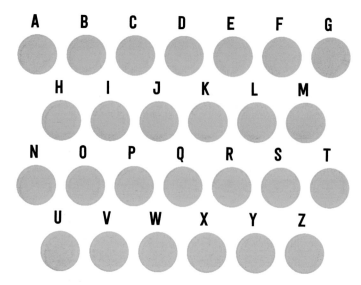

$\overline{}_{1} \overline{}_{2} \overline{}_{3} \overline{}_{4} \overline{}_{5} \qquad \overline{}_{6} \overline{}_{7} \overline{}_{8}$

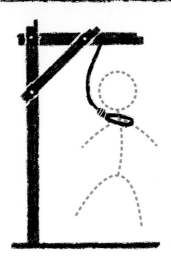

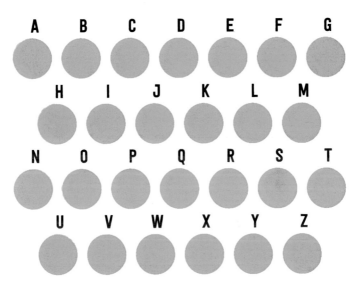

A B C D E F G

H I J K L M

N O P Q R S T

U V W X Y Z

‾ ‾ ‾ ‾ ‾ ‾   ‾ ‾ ‾
1 2 3 4 5 6   7 8 9

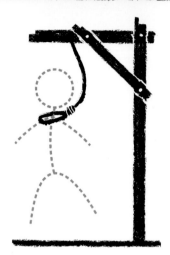

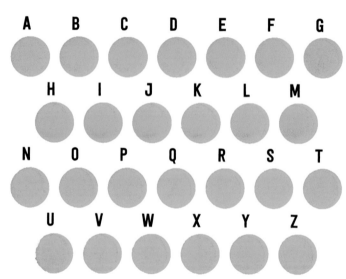

A B C D E F G

H I J K L M

N O P Q R S T

U V W X Y Z

$\overline{}$ $\overline{}$ $\overline{}$ $\overline{}$ $\overline{}$ $\overline{}$ $\overline{}$ $\overline{}$ $\overline{}$ $\overline{}$
1   2   3   4   5   6   7   8   9   10

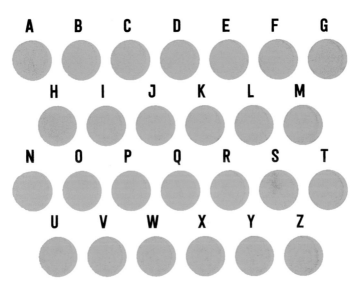

A B C D E F G

H I J K L M

N O P Q R S T

U V W X Y Z

$\overline{\quad}_{1}$ $\overline{\quad}_{2}$ $\overline{\quad}_{3}$ $\overline{\quad}_{4}$ $\overline{\quad}_{5}$ $\overline{\quad}_{6}$ $\overline{\quad}_{7}$ $\overline{\quad}_{8}$

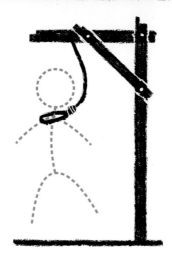

A B C D E F G

H I J K L M

N O P Q R S T

U V W X Y Z

$$\overline{}\ \overline{}\ \overline{}\ \overline{}\ \overline{}\ \overline{}\ \overline{}$$
1 2 3 4 5 6 7